Living LARGE

An Elephant's Life

Sara Antill

Prospect Heights Public Library
12 N Elm Street
Prospect Heights, IL 60070
www.phpl.info

New York

Published in 2012 by The Rosen Publishing Group, Inc.
29 East 21st Street, New York, NY 10010

Copyright © 2012 by The Rosen Publishing Group, Inc.

All rights reserved. No part of this book may be reproduced in any form without permission in writing from the publisher, except by a reviewer.

First Edition

Editor: Jennifer Way
Book Design: Greg Tucker

Photo Credits: Cover, pp. 4, 5, 6, 7, 8 (left, right), 10, 11 (left, right), 12 (top, bottom), 13, 14 (top, bottom), 15 (bottom), 16, 17, 18, 19, 20 Shutterstock.com; p. 15 (top) iStockphoto/Thinkstock; p. 21 Ben Cranke/Getty Images; p. 22 © Gregory Tucker.

Library of Congress Cataloging-in-Publication Data

Antill, Sara.
 An elephant's life / by Sara Antill. — 1st ed.
    p. cm. — (Living large)
 Includes index.
 ISBN 978-1-4488-4979-6 (library binding) — ISBN 978-1-4488-5106-5 (pbk.) — ISBN 978-1-4488-5107-2 (6-pack)
 1. Elephants—Life cycles—Juvenile literature. I. Title.
 QL737.P98A584 2012
 599.67'156—dc22
                              2010050513

Manufactured in the United States of America

CPSIA Compliance Information: Batch #WS11PK: For Further Information contact Rosen Publishing, New York, New York at 1-800-237-9932

Contents

Meet the Elephant	4
Elephant Species	6
Many Different Homes	8
Not Just a Nose!	10
Living Together	12
Life Cycle of an Elephant	14
Trunk in Training	16
Growing Up	18
Big Families	20
Elephants in Danger	22
Glossary	23
Index	24
Web Sites	24

Meet the Elephant

Have you ever seen an elephant in the wild or in a zoo? If so, you likely noticed that elephants are really big! In fact, elephants are the largest land animals on Earth. Have you ever wondered what an elephant's life is like?

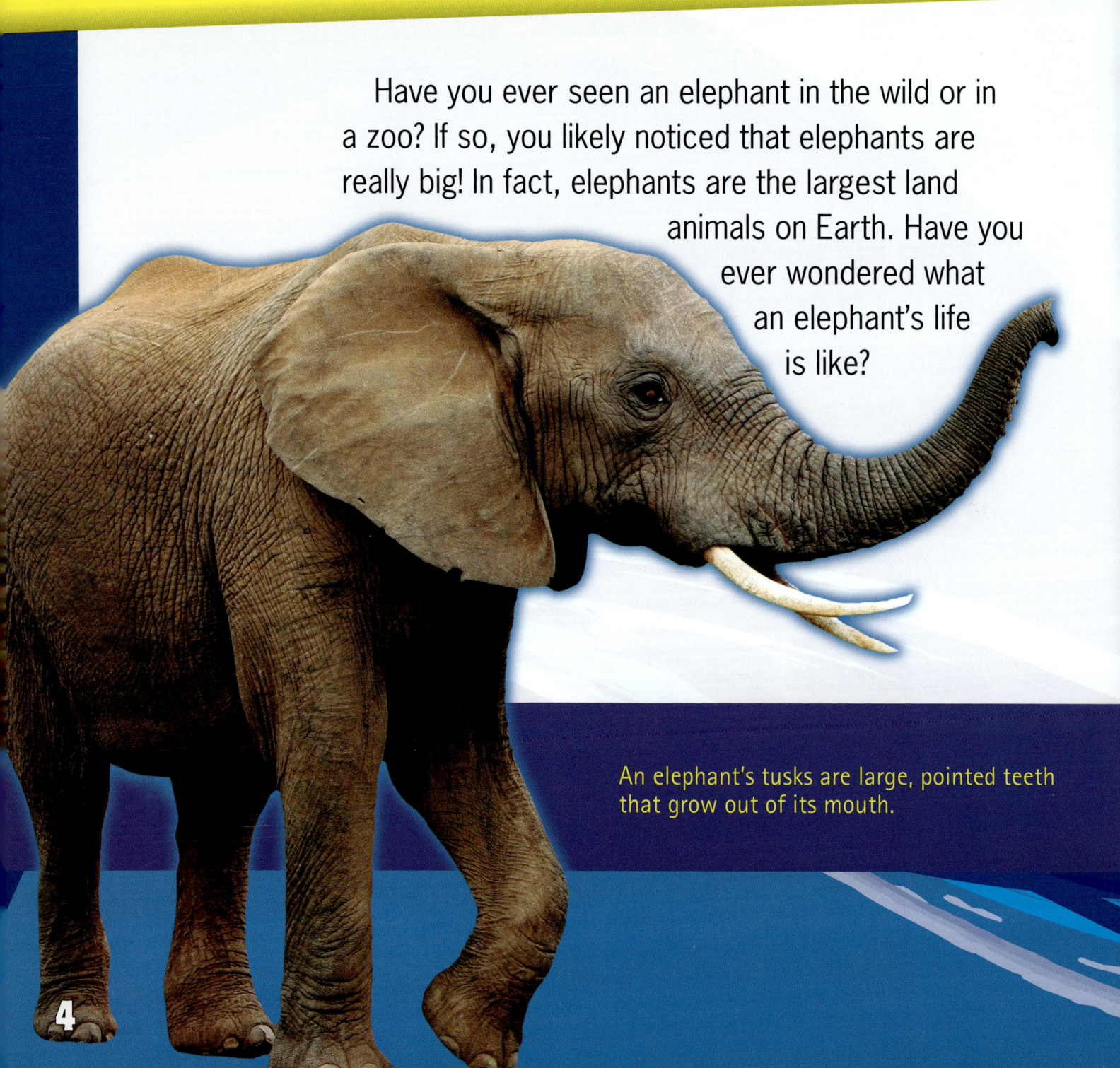

An elephant's tusks are large, pointed teeth that grow out of its mouth.

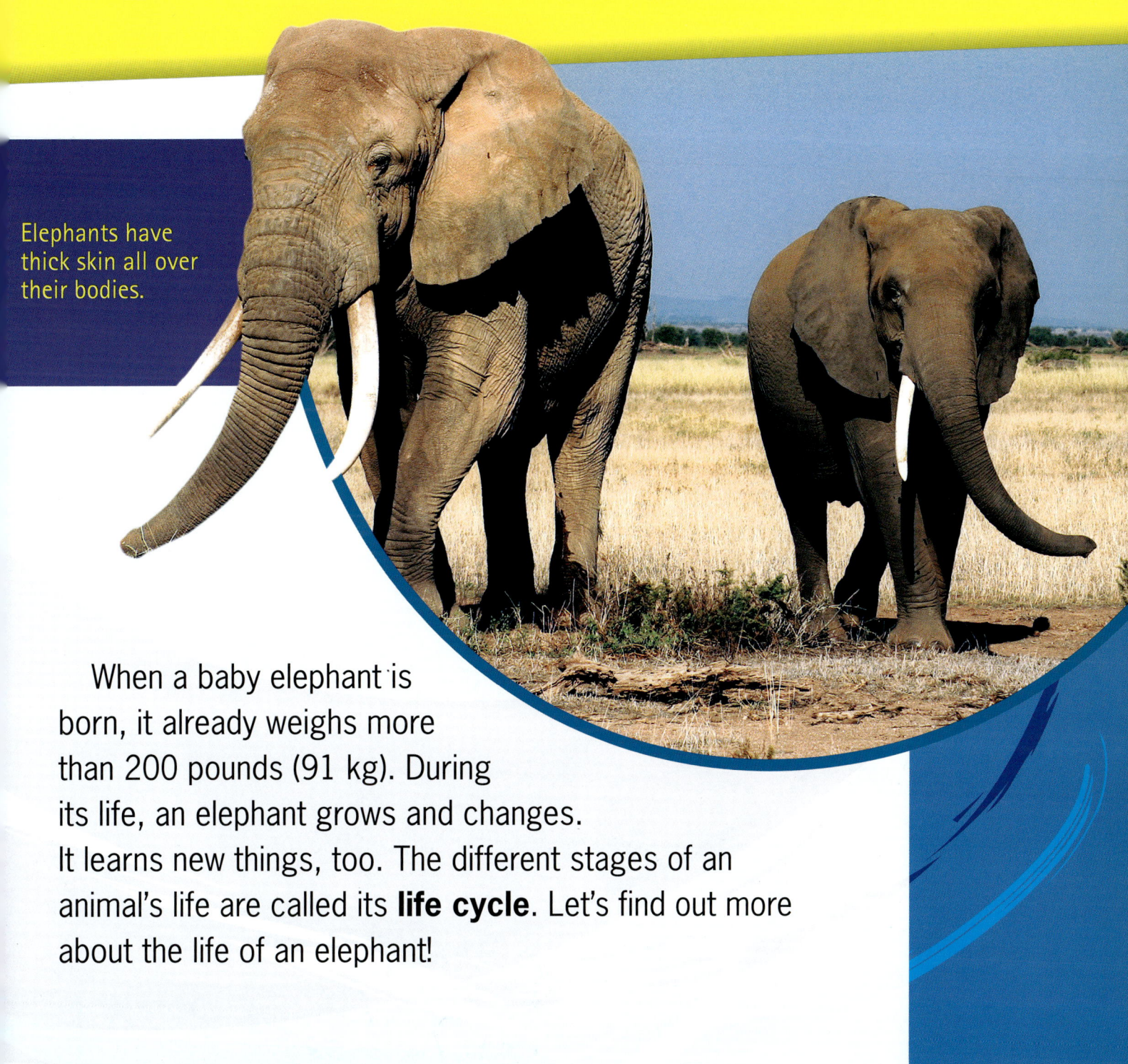

Elephants have thick skin all over their bodies.

When a baby elephant is born, it already weighs more than 200 pounds (91 kg). During its life, an elephant grows and changes. It learns new things, too. The different stages of an animal's life are called its **life cycle**. Let's find out more about the life of an elephant!

Elephant Species

There are two major groupings of elephants. Two **species** of African elephants live in Africa. Asian elephants are the species that lives in Asia. That is not the only difference between them, though. Both species of African elephants can grow to be 14 feet (4 m) tall and nearly 30 feet (9 m) long. They can weigh up to 15,000 pounds (6,804 kg).

The two species of African elephants are the African forest elephant and the African savanna elephant. Savannas are grasslands. This picture shows African savanna elephants.

Another difference between the Asian elephant and the African elephants is their ears. Asian elephants have smaller ears, like the one shown here.

Asian elephants are a little smaller. They generally stand less than 10 feet (3 m) tall and can grow to be 21 feet (6 m) long. Asian elephants can weigh up to 11,000 pounds (4,990 kg).

Many Different Homes

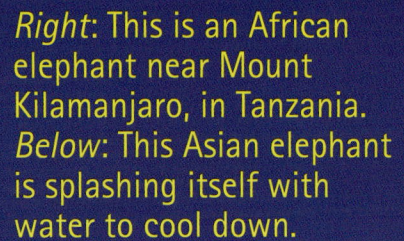

Right: This is an African elephant near Mount Kilamanjaro, in Tanzania.
Below: This Asian elephant is splashing itself with water to cool down.

Elephants live in many different types of **habitats**. All they need is enough food, water, and space to move around. African elephant species live all across Africa, from the thick rain forests and savannas to deserts. Asian elephants can live in low, wet forests or dry, cool mountain forests thousands of miles (km) high.

Elephants are **herbivores**, which means they eat only plants. The types of plants they eat depend on where they live. Most elephants eat a mix of grasses, leaves, fruit, and twigs. An adult elephant can eat more than 300 pounds (136 kg) of food in one day!

Where Asian Elephants Live

Key
Asian elephant range

Asia

Pacific Ocean

Indian Ocean

Australia

The Asian elephant's range is shown in yellow.

9

Not Just a Nose!

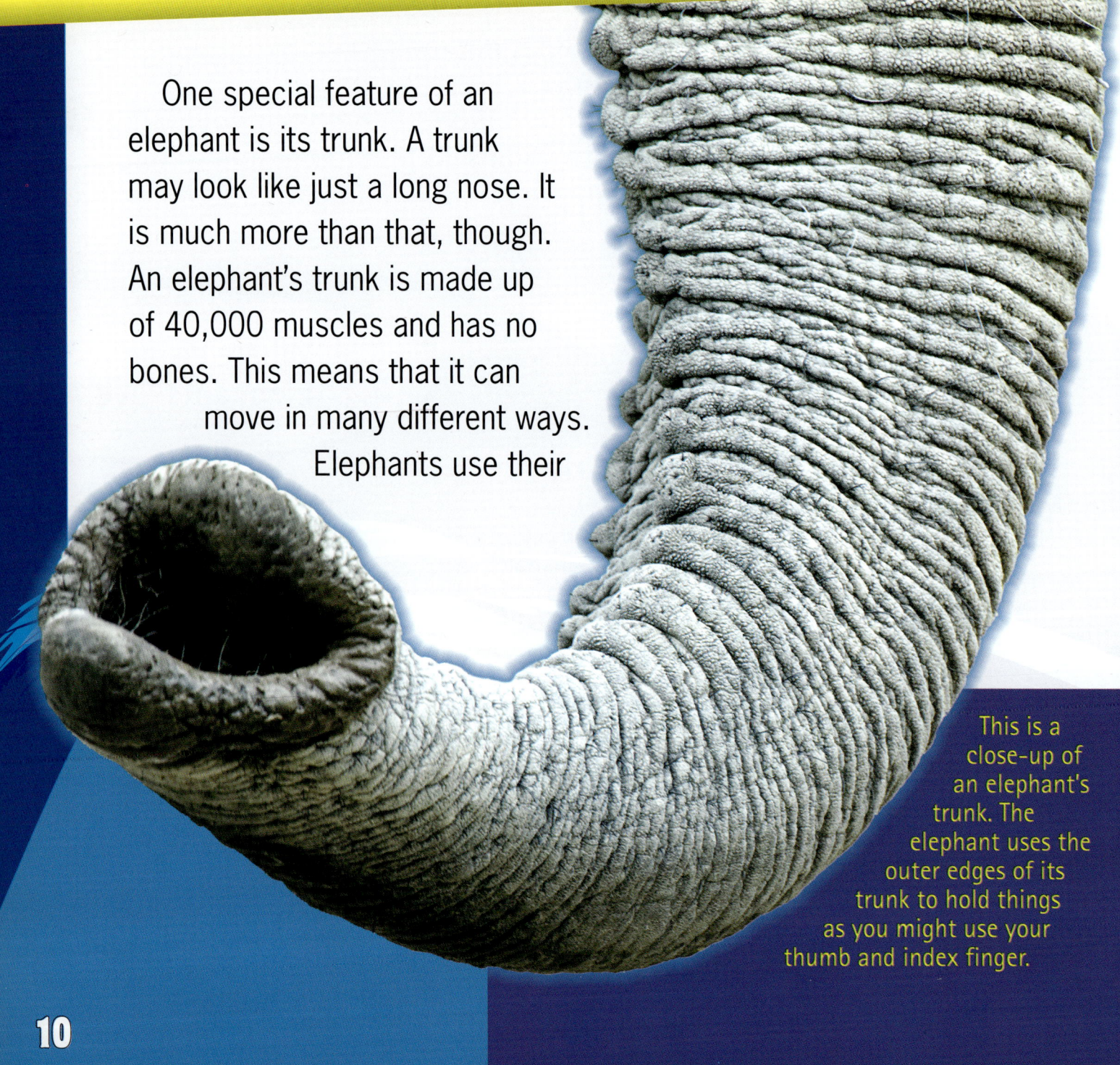

One special feature of an elephant is its trunk. A trunk may look like just a long nose. It is much more than that, though. An elephant's trunk is made up of 40,000 muscles and has no bones. This means that it can move in many different ways. Elephants use their

This is a close-up of an elephant's trunk. The elephant uses the outer edges of its trunk to hold things as you might use your thumb and index finger.

trunks to smell, pick up food, and greet each other.

An elephant also uses its trunk to dig in the ground for water. It can then suck the water into its trunk, point the trunk into its mouth, and blow! The water shoots into the elephant's mouth.

Top: An elephant's trunk helps it draw up water for drinking or spraying. *Left*: Here is an elephant using its trunk to eat cactus leaves.

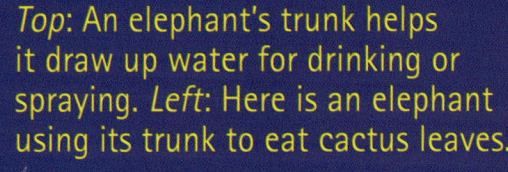

Living Together

Elephants are very smart animals. They play with each other and hug each other with their trunks. Most elephants live in family groups, called **herds**. A herd is generally led by an older female and has between 10 and 20 members. The group can include young elephants,

Top: When a herd is on the move, the young are kept near the middle so that they will be safer.
Bottom: Elephants sometimes twist their trunks together as a friendly greeting to each other.

mothers, sisters, and cousins of different ages.

Elephants speak to each other using deep growling noises. In fact, elephants can tell each other apart by their different growls. They can also make very loud, sharp noises with their trunks. This lets other elephants know that there is danger nearby.

A herd does many things together. This herd is stopping for a drink of water.

Life Cycle of an Elephant

1 A baby elephant weighs between 200 and 250 pounds (91–113 kg) when it is born. Its mother will use her trunk to help the baby to its feet. Baby elephants spend the first months of their lives learning to use their trunks.

4 Most female elephants give birth to one baby at a time. When a baby is born, many females in the herd will help raise it. The baby will drink its mother's milk until she gives birth again.

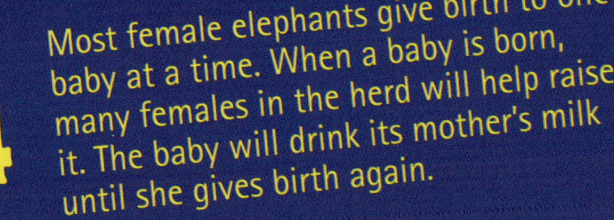

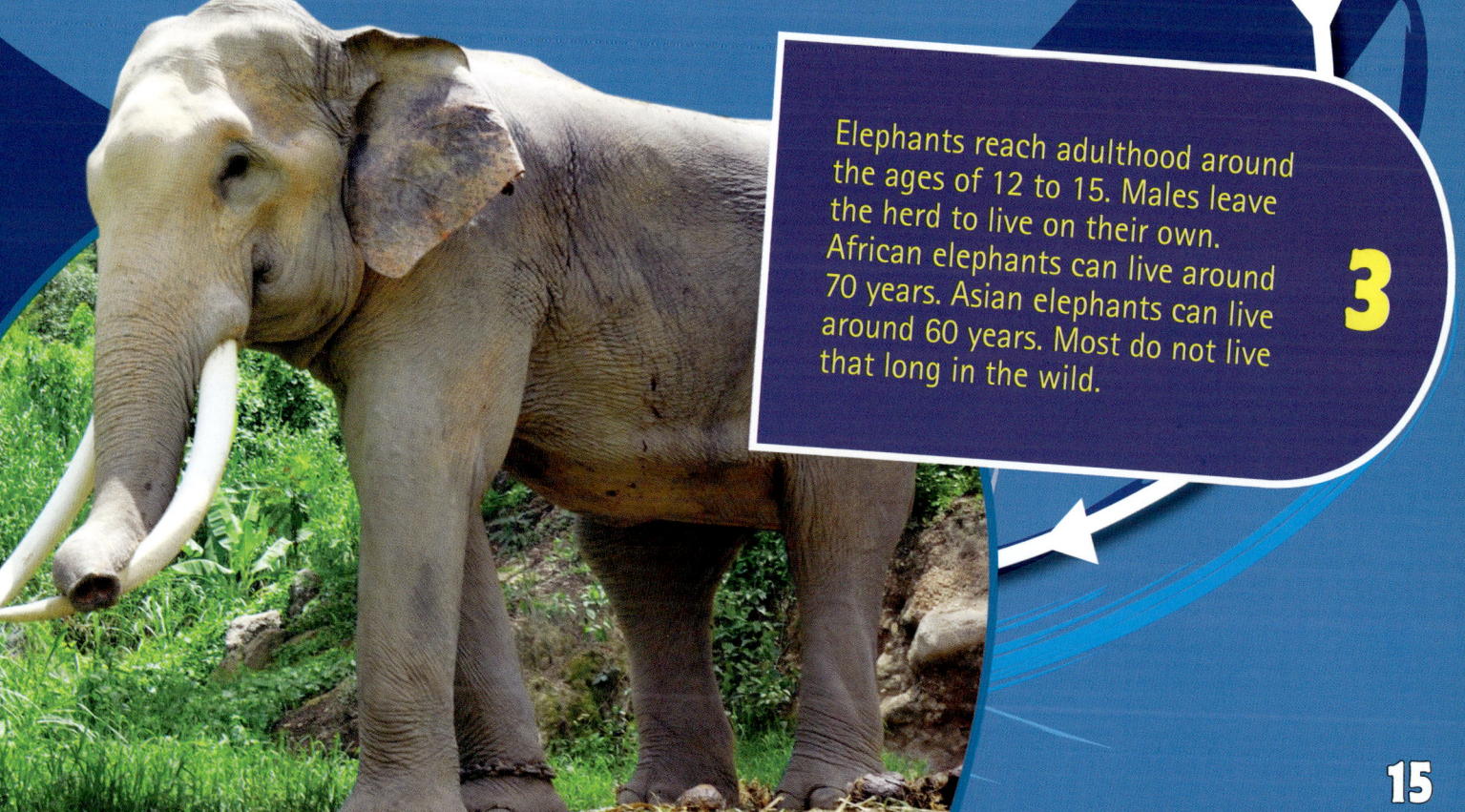

2 By the age of five, young elephants can weigh around 2,000 pounds (907 kg). They are ready to start finding their own food. Around the age of six, young males will start to wander away from the herd for short periods of time. Young females stay closer to their mothers.

3 Elephants reach adulthood around the ages of 12 to 15. Males leave the herd to live on their own. African elephants can live around 70 years. Asian elephants can live around 60 years. Most do not live that long in the wild.

Trunk in Training

Elephants are **mammals**. As all mammals do, elephants feed their young milk from their bodies. A baby elephant is called a **calf**. Newborn calves weigh around 200 to 250 pounds (91–113 kg).

A calf cannot control the muscles in its trunk until it is a few months old. Until that time, the calf will drink its

Elephant calves often suck the ends of their trunks the way human babies suck their thumbs!

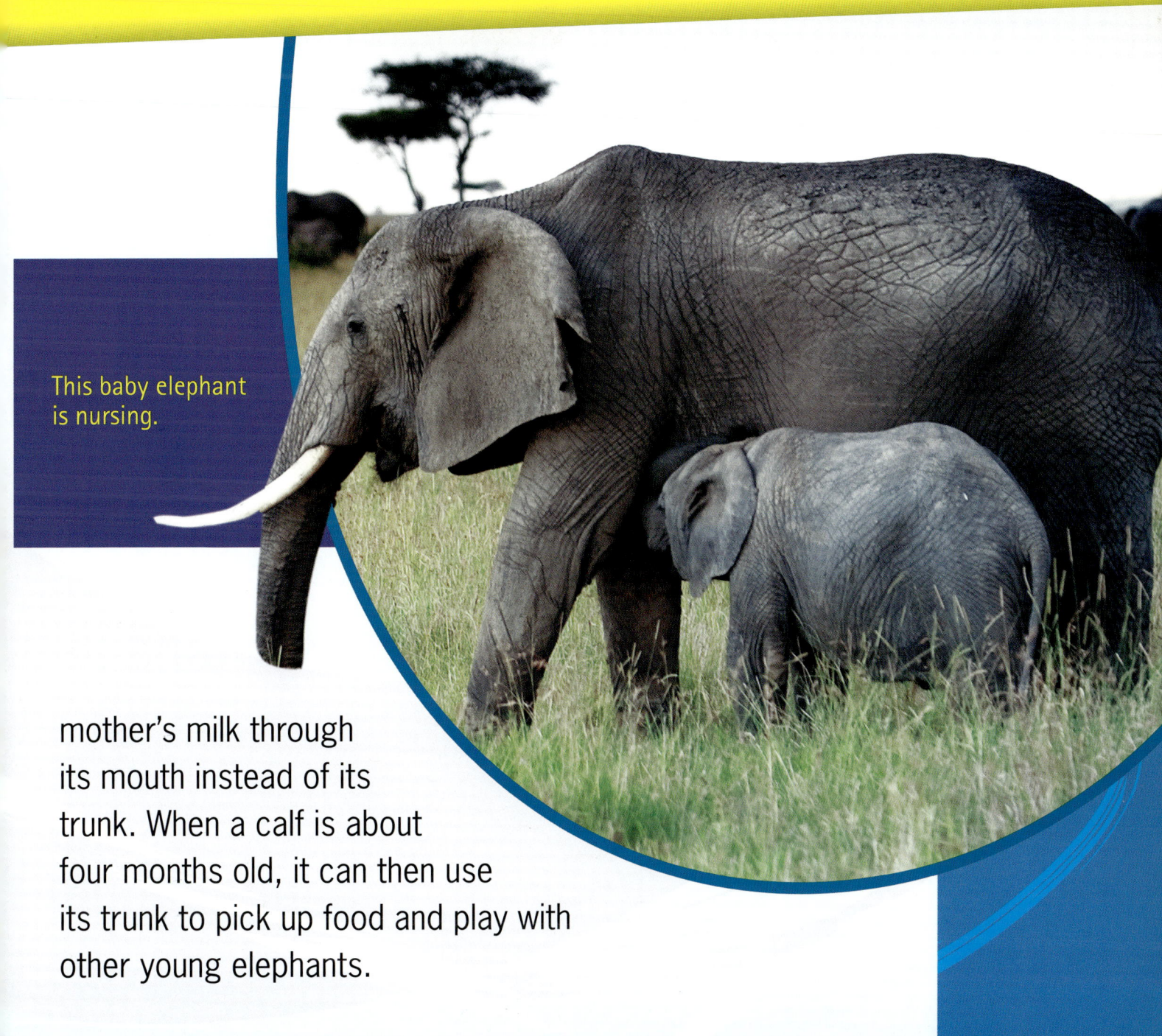

This baby elephant is nursing.

mother's milk through its mouth instead of its trunk. When a calf is about four months old, it can then use its trunk to pick up food and play with other young elephants.

Growing Up

When a calf is around five years old, its mother often has another baby on the way. This means that it is time for the calf to be **weaned**. Young elephants start learning new skills, like finding food, by watching the older members of the herd.

As young elephants get a little older, they spend more time away from their mothers.

At around 12 to 15 years old, elephants are full grown. A male elephant will leave its family group and live the rest of its life either alone or with other males. Female elephants tend to stay in the herds where they were born.

Elephants spread dirt and mud on their skin. This helps cool them down and keeps their skin safe from bug bites and sunburn.

Big Families

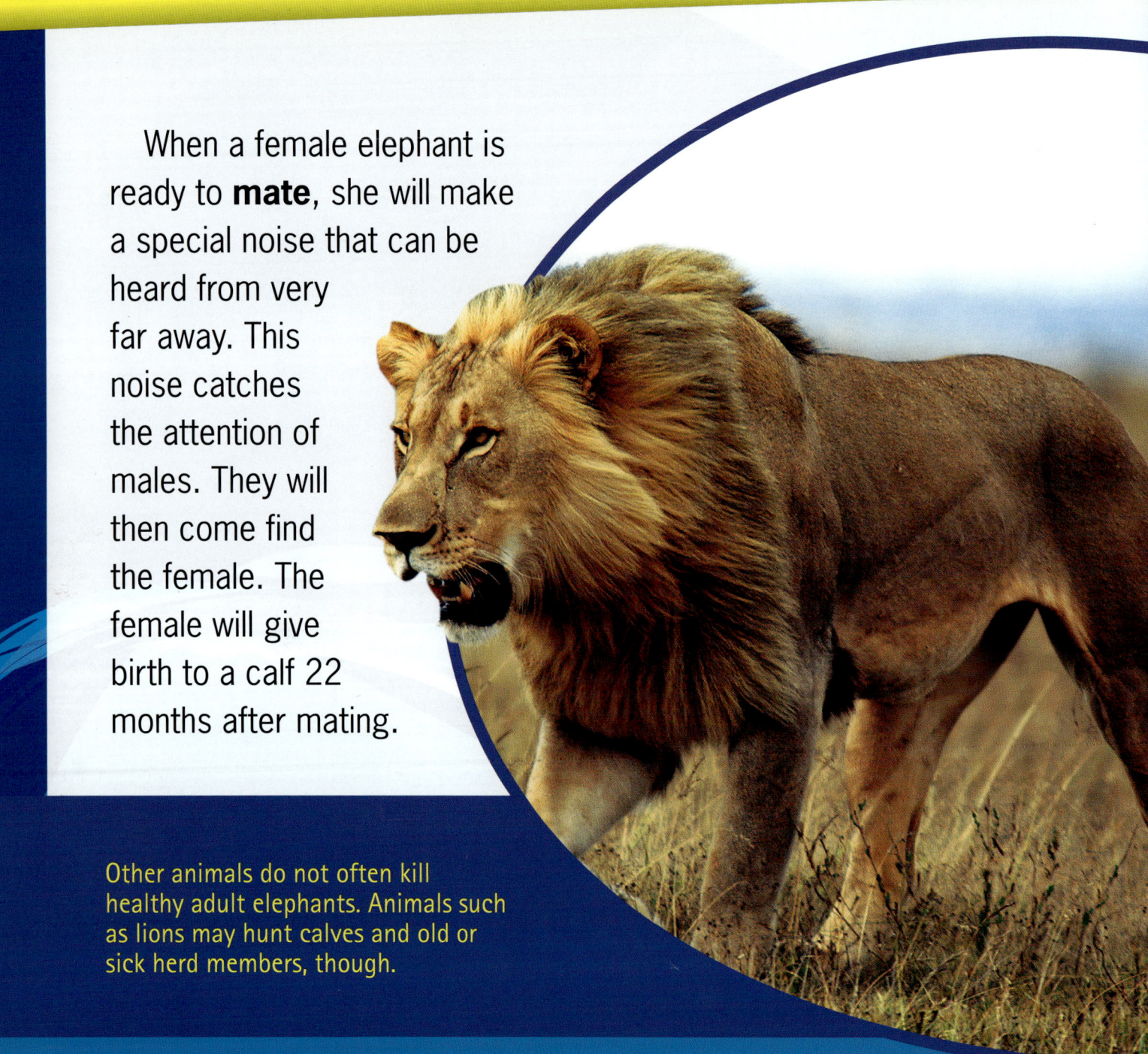

When a female elephant is ready to **mate**, she will make a special noise that can be heard from very far away. This noise catches the attention of males. They will then come find the female. The female will give birth to a calf 22 months after mating.

Other animals do not often kill healthy adult elephants. Animals such as lions may hunt calves and old or sick herd members, though.

Often, the other young female elephants in a herd will help a mother raise her calf. These young females are called **allomothers**. This extra help keeps the young calf safe and well cared for. It also helps the allomothers learn how to take care of their own calves when they are older.

Elephants use their trunks to bond with other members of the herd by stroking each other.

Elephants in Danger

For thousands of years, people used elephants for hard work because of their size and strength. However, in the last 100 years, the number of elephants in the world has dropped by more than half. This is due to habitat loss and **poaching**. Some people continue to hunt elephants for their **tusks**, which can be worth a lot of money.

Many people are trying to save elephants. They are trying to stop people from building homes and cities on land where elephants live. We can all help by not buying things made from elephant tusks.

Asian elephants have long been used to carry people, much as horses have.

Glossary

allomothers (A-loh-muh-therz) Young female elephants that help other females raise their calves.

calf (KAF) A baby elephant.

habitats (HA-buh-tats) The kinds of land where animals or plants naturally live.

herbivores (ER-buh-vorz) Animals that eat only plants.

herds (HURDZ) Groups of the same kind of animals living together.

life cycle (LYF SY-kul) The stages in an animal's life, from birth to death.

mammals (MA-mulz) Warm-blooded animals that have backbones and hair, breathe air, and feed milk to their young.

mate (MAYT) To come together to make babies.

poaching (POHCH-ing) Hunting animals when it is against the law.

species (SPEE-sheez) One kind of living thing. All people are one species.

tusks (TUSKS) Long, large pointed teeth that come out of the mouths of some animals.

weaned (WEEND) Changed a baby's food from a mother's milk to solid food.

Index

A
Africa, 6, 8
Asia, 6

C
calf, 16–18, 20–21

D
deserts, 8
difference, 6

E
Earth, 4

F
food, 8–9, 11, 15, 17–18
forests, 8–9

H
habitats, 8
herbivores, 9
herd(s), 12, 14–15, 18–19, 21

L
life cycle, 5

M
mammals, 16

N
noise(s), 13, 20

P
plants, 9

R
rain forests, 8

S
savannas, 8
space, 8
stages, 5

T
types, 8–9

W
water, 8, 11
wild, 4, 15

Z
zoo, 4

Web Sites

Due to the changing nature of Internet links, PowerKids Press has developed an online list of Web sites related to the subject of this book. This site is updated regularly. Please use this link to access the list: www.powerkidslinks.com/livl/elephant/

Prospect Heights Public Library
12 N. Elm Street
Prospect Heights, IL 60070
www.phpl.info